HOW TO CLEAN YOUR LAPTOP

To Prevent Overheating

A Do It Yourself Guide for All to Use

Complete Step By Step Guide including disassembly instructions for any model laptop.

All laptop and notebook computers will at some point need to be cleaned. This will prevent overheating and will prevent future component failure. Thermal damage is the number one reason that laptops fail and break down.

I will start by discussing how to disassemble your laptop (this will show you how to disassemble any laptop). I will show you the tools and supplies needed for a proper cleaning. Then, once your laptop is apart, I will instruct you how to properly clean all internal components bringing your laptop back to "like new" condition and back to running "cool".

These instructions are for everyone to use, you don't have to be technically inclined to clean your laptop. I will walk you through the whole process to ensure you have done a precise and professional job.

Tools and Supplies Needed:

Mini Flat-Head Screwdriver (like found in an eyeglass repair kit)

1

Small Phillips-Head Screwdriver (a multi tip screwdriver will work best) <- slightly smaller than the average Household screwdriver

Note: Apple Laptops use a Star Tip Screw- so buying a multi tip mini screwdriver set will give you a few of these tips in various sizes.

1 Earth Magnet (Radio Shack sells these) ← optional

Note: you place this small magnet on your screwdriver tip to magnetize it which will allow each screw to stick to the tip when removing them from the laptop case parts.

1 Toothbrush (soft or medium bristles)

Q-tips or Cotton Swabs ← optional

Paper Towels

Windex or similar Glass Cleaning Solution

Circuit Board Cleaner (Radio Shack sells this) ← optional

2oz water cups (to hold screws of various sizes, which will keep them separated by size)

Guitar Pick or similar thin plastic object/tool ← optional

5 min. Plastic Weld Epoxy (auto zone or similar auto markets will sell this) ← optional

Note: The epoxy would only be needed if you happen to have broken screw posts on the inside of the laptops bottom or upper casing.

WD-40

That's it! Now you're ready to disassemble.

Complete Disassembly of the Laptop Instructions

To start, you will begin by placing the bottom side up. Now that you have the laptop upside down, you will remove the battery. To remove the battery, most laptops will have sliding levers to unlock the battery and release it to remove. Some laptops will have the battery screwed down (Apple and HP have some that do). Most will have 2 levers and some will have only one. If there are 2, one of them is usually the locking lever and the other is the release lever. You should see an imprinted icon or instructions near each lever to instruct you on how to slide or unlock the levers. Pull the battery up or slide it out and remove, set aside.

Now you will use your mini Phillips-head screwdriver to remove all the screws from the bottom case of the laptop. Start at the rear and work your way around to the front. Keyboard screws will have a keyboard icon next to them. The optical drive will have a CD icon next to it. There will usually be some type of cover or covers on the bottom of the laptop (ram cover, hard drive cover, Wi-Fi card cover etc…) which you will unscrew the screws on them and pry the covers away (the mini flat head screwdriver works best to aid in removal of the covers). The hard drive is the large rectangular component (some will not be visible yet or some are located on the upper side of the motherboard. Note; the Motherboard is the large green or blue circuit board inside the laptop.

Look in the empty battery bay, there are usually screws there that need to be removed.

Notice that most laptops will use a few different size screws on the bottom of the laptop, I will explain.

The sizes will vary from laptop to laptop. The thing to remember is where the smaller ones go. The screws in the battery bay area will usually be smaller screws… Set these aside in a small cup or holder and label them to remember where they go.

Now, the rear of the laptop (near the hinges) will usually have the longest screws. Like the screws holding the hinge plates and the upper screen… These will be longer. The keyboard screws tend to be long as well, just as long as the rear ones. Put these in cups and label them. Set aside…

Look for screws securing the hard drive (if visible) and remove them. Now remove the hard drive. To remove the hard drive, most will slide away from the Plug-in Port. Others will lift away with a small plug that attaches to the motherboard. These plugs will have a Pull Tab on them. You simply pull upward and the plug will release from its port on the motherboard. Some laptops will have Dual Hard drives – which both then need to be removed.

The RAM (memory) chips can stay in their slots.

Unplug the 2 or 3 Wi-Fi wires from the card (usually a black and a white wire, sometimes there is a gray and/or a blue) and if the Wi-Fi card is attached by a screw or 2 screws, then remove the screws and pull the card upward and outward to remove it from the slide-in port on the motherboard.

Some Wi-Fi cards will have long antenna wires that travel along the bottom case to a hole going to the upper side of the laptop. You want to un-track these wires so you can readily pull them from the upper side of the laptop (palm-rest area). This is a good time to look for any other wires that are running along the bottom base, and unplug them if needed to remove the casing. Most CMOS batteries can be left alone, if you do find that your CMOS battery (looks like a nickel) is sitting in a plastic tray, you should unstick it from the tray so that you are able to pull the motherboard away from the bottom base without ripping the CMOS battery and plug from its port.

Now look for the CD icon screw... Remove it if you can find it. If you can't find it, I will describe where you will find the location of it. The optical drive is a large square shape - so you will look where the end of the optical drive is (the front being the face plate with the eject button and such...) and the center of the end of the drive is where the screw is located. It's mainly towards the center of the laptop (in the middle)... Once you have found and removed the CD drive (optical drive) screw, you will need to slide the optical drive out and away from the laptop. To do this, use your mini flat head screwdriver or guitar pick and place the tip between the drives face plate and the bottom base of the laptop and pull outward to slide the drive out and away from the laptops bottom base. Once removed; place it off to the side, now look at the molding of the bottom base area where you removed the optical drive. You are looking for any screws there to remove. These screws are going to be small ones that are used to secure the bottom base to the upper base (palm rest area). Remove and place in a labeled cup.

Look in the empty hard drive bay area(s) for any screws as these will typically be smaller ones too... Now when I say smaller, I mean shorter... the size (around) is usually the same for all the screws on your laptop.

Another good idea to do is use a camera or cell phone to snap photos of your disassembly process, this way you can just reverse the process using your photos when reassembling the laptop.

You want to finish removing all screws from the bottom of the laptop.

Some laptops will require that you now remove the fan and heat-sink assembly if it is visible from the bottom side of laptop. Certain models like the Dell Inspiron 1545 will have the heat-sink on the bottom of the laptop and in order to remove the bottom base, you first need to remove the fan and heat-sink assembly (first unplugging the fan from its port on the motherboard).

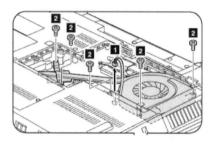

You should now have all the screws removed from the bottom of the laptop...

The next step is going to vary for your specific laptop model.

Some laptops like the Sony Vaio or Samsung laptops will have the motherboard attached to the palm-rest so your next step will be to pull the bottom base casing away from the laptop. Do this by grabbing an area like the optical drive bay, then pull it upward to un snap it from the upper palm-rest. If you come across resistance, look for any screws you might have missed.

Most other models will require you to now flip the laptop over to remove the keyboard and palm-rest to get access to the motherboard. These laptops have the motherboard secured to the bottom base as opposed to the ones previously discussed that have the motherboard secured to the palm-rest.

You will start from the upper area (assuming you have the laptop in front of you with the screen opened). You will start at the area just above the keyboard. Most model laptops have a "media strip" or some kind of separate molding piece that runs along the whole top of the keyboard. This is probably still held on by snaps so you will use your Pry tool now to "pop" the media strip or molding up and away from the laptop. Be careful here because some model laptops have fragile ribbon wires or cables that run from the molding strip to the motherboard. Use your guitar pick or mini flat head screwdriver to help you lift this molding piece away.

If you do find that the molding/media strip does have ribbon cable attached, you will need to disconnect the cable/wire. Most will use a locking lever, either a lift up one or a slide out one. The lift up ones will have a small tab on the top that you will pry up with the mini flat head screwdriver. The other type, the slide out type will have 2 plastic tabs usually yellow/tan in color. You will again use the flathead screwdriver and pull the tab outward on each end of the ribbon cable where it enters the port. They slide out about a millimeter (don't over slide it by pulling it out too far or it will break) then pull the ribbon wire away from the port.

Some laptops will have a secondary molding piece that wraps around the outside of the keyboard. You will now use your pry tool and lift the molding piece upward starting at one of the sides of the keyboard. These molding pieces are just held in by plastic snaps and should easily unsnap for removal. A typical model that uses these is the Dell Studio series HP does too.

On models like the IBM ThinkPad, you will have to first remove the molding piece below the keyboard. This piece can be removed by using your pry tool at the top – middle of the palm-rest (just below the keyboard) lifting upward, the bottom piece will then lift away.

Some models have a fingerprint reader on them, so when pulling the molding piece away be careful and look for a ribbon cable attachment, remove the cable if needed. There will also be a "pull away" cable going from the bottom of the center of the palm-rest (touchpad) that snaps onto its corresponding plug port on the motherboard. Go slow and watch for these two things.

Now you want to look for any screws securing the bottom of the keyboard to the laptop, remove them (usually 4 if any). Remove keyboard if able, set aside. Now remove the upper molding that lies around the upper part of where the keyboard is/was. Unscrew the screws (usually marked) and pull the upper piece away.

Note: make sure you keep separating your screws into little cups with labels.

Now back to the other model laptops. We left off with the removal of the upper molding piece or the media strip.

You will now be able to remove the keyboard securing screws (usually 4) at the top of the keyboard.

Once removed, you will lift the keyboard up and away lifting it from the top of the keyboard. Only lift it to a perpendicular position (90 degree angle), because you will have a wide ribbon cable that goes from the bottom middle of the keyboard and attaches to the motherboard. This too will have a locking lever tab on the motherboard keyboard port that you will need to pry up or pry outward on both tab ends to release the keyboard cable from the motherboard port. Some keyboards will have a smaller secondary cable attaching to a locking lever port on the motherboard; this cable is usually the backlight cable for your keyboard and will need to be carefully removed from its port.

You should now have the keyboard removed.

If not, you might have a newer laptop that requires you to start the upper disassembly process by first removing the keyboard. These are the thinner, more streamlined laptops and are usually the metal frame/base laptops. You will use your pry tool here and begin by looking for any tabs that are securing the keyboard tray in its place. Laptops with these tabs will have 4 of them they will be black in color and you will use your mini flat head screwdriver to push them inward to unlock the keyboard tab and release it. These spring-loaded tabs can be quite a pain to push in and keep in. You have to start at one and continue on pushing each other of the 4 tabs in, while doing this you want to also use a secondary pry tool to try and lift the keyboard tray away from the laptop at the top of the keyboard.

Once the top of the keyboard is freed, you can disconnect the ribbon cable from the motherboard and remove the keyboard. Some laptops will have simple slide tabs (like the HP NC series) and will still usually have 4 of them. Sony Vaio uses these too. You simply use your pry tool and pull down on each tab to un-slide it from the lock – pulling downward.

You will now have the keyboard removed for most to all models. You will now need to look in the empty keyboard bay area to remove any screws. These screws are usually labeled (they will have the size number or an arrow) and you will also need to unplug any ribbon cables or wires from the motherboard that are visible. These cables or wires are usually speaker wires, power button wires or cable etc… and you will need to disconnect the display cable and un-track the Wi-Fi cables to allow you to remove the upper screen from the bottom base.

Some laptops will have a screw that is securing the optical drive in place (you will notice you were not able to remove the DVD drive as earlier instructed to do), remove the screw and now slide the optical drive encasement out and away from the laptop, set aside.

Let me explain here about the removal process of the Display Cable.

These cables will vary in connection types.

Some will plug in straight up and down,

Some will plug in from the side and secured with a piece of clear or black tape,

Some will plug in and will have a "pull tab" to pull them upward and away,

Be careful here; go slow when removing these cables.

If you're able to remove the palm-rest now, do so.

You might need to pry it upward with your pry tool due to plastic retaining snaps around the outer edge of most laptops connecting the palm-rest to the bottom base.

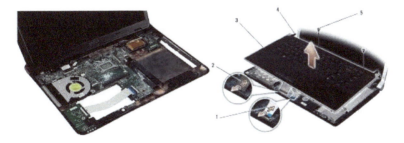

Some laptops require you to first remove the screen before removing the palm-rest. To remove the screen, you need to unscrew the hinges from the hinge posts on the bottom base.

There are usually 2 per side, sometimes more. When you have all the screws removed, pull the screen away and make sure to gently free the cables and wires coming from either side of the lower screen hinge area. These cables/wires will be the display cable, the Wi-Fi wires, webcam cable, microphone cable etc… though usually you will have just the display cable on one side and two antenna wires on the opposite side.

Note: you will not disassemble your actual screen like the photo above; it is just a reference for the removal of entire upper screen portion.

By now you will hopefully have the screen removed and the upper palm-rest removed from the laptop. You will now see in front of you; the Motherboard.

Something similar to the above photo…

You will first need to unplug any cables or remove any remaining wires. Some laptops will have a modem wire with a plug that needs to be unplugged and pulled away from the area. Sometimes you can pull the plug right out and sometimes you have to unscrew the card and lift it up and away from its port on the motherboard to allow access for removal of the wire plug.

MOTHERBOARD REMOVAL

Some motherboards will have screws holding them down to the bottom base and some laptops do not, though most do.

The screws that need to be removed will be marked on the motherboard either with numbers or with arrows. Remove all of them; they usually follow the outer edge of the motherboard with 2 or 3 being in the center.

The motherboard should now be free to be removed from the bottom base. Double-check to ensure that all cables and wires attached to the motherboard are now disconnected and away from the motherboard immediate area.

When lifting the motherboard out and away from the bottom base, you want to be careful of the Wi-Fi switch if there is one, also look out for a volume knob/disc as you

13

will need to pull the board away from these ports first and then lift upward. Look where the VGA port is (if you have one) and pull the motherboard away from these ports on the base (usually near the fan).

Note: Some laptops require you to unscrew the fan from the bottom base, so look here for any screws attaching the fan to the base and remove them.

Remove Motherboard.

Now back to the laptops that have the motherboard attached to the upper palm-rest (like the Sony Vaio and Samsung). You now should have the bottom base pulled away from the laptop and the laptop is in the folded closed position in front of you with the bottom-side up facing you - as you see the motherboard in front of you. With these models you now have everything that needs to be cleaned exposed. There is no need for keyboard or palm-rest removal with these models.

The Cleaning Process Begins

Cleaning the Fan and Heat-Sink

You will see the fan and heat-sink assembly on the motherboard. Remove the retaining screws and unplug the fan from the motherboard (gently). Pull the heat-sink and fan away from the motherboard. If the fan is separate from the heat-sink, unscrew the fan completely and remove it, you might need to pull a tape strip or two to remove the fan from the heat-sink.

You will now have just the fan and heat-sink in front of you, set every other part aside for now.

Most will look similar to this... Unless you have already removed the fan and you just have a separate heat-sink.

Assuming you have one that resembles the photo here, I will discuss the cleaning process of this type.

You will start by looking for the Micro screws that secure the fan base to the upper plate (there are usually 4 of these).

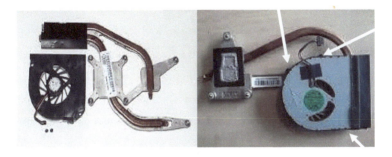

You will find on some laptops (along with the micro screws) some securing tape strips that secure the top plate of the fan to the base of the fan housing. This tape will be black, gray or silver, just cut it or rip/peel it to remove. You should now have the fan itself exposed. Most laptop fans will use a magnetic motor. These fans can be removed. You simply grab a hold of the blades and lift upward with a slight wiggle when lifting and it will come right off the motor. Some fans will not be removable as they are attached to the motor post.

To clean the fan, you will use the toothbrush. You will also be using paper towels here.

You start with a dry bristled toothbrush. Brush gently in between the fan blades all the way around the fan. Then take a piece of paper towel and fold it a few times to give it some thickness. Spray it with a little cleaning solution (Windex or similar) and slide it in and out of each fan blade area to clean both sides of the blades. Then use the dry toothbrush once again to go over the blades and in between them. Use the toothbrush on the fan motor and base as well, cleaning every area thoroughly. You can use the damp paper towel here too. Now you can put the fan back onto its motor… To do this, you line up the fan post with the hole in the center of the fan motor and slide it on. That is it. Now reassemble the fan the same way you disassembled it. Put the top and bottom together and screw in the 4 micro screws to secure the top of the fan to the bottom base of the fan. Test the fan for adequate movement by spinning it with your finger. It should spin freely, if it doesn't then you need to check if the top fan plate is rubbing against the blades and if it is, use your pry tool and lift the plate center rim upward and in a circular motion around the center circle opening. This should free the fan and allow it to spin properly.

Take the heat-sink and flip it over to expose the thermal paste and thermal pads.

You can now replace the thermal paste and or thermal pads.

Most of the time the current thermal paste will be sufficient and there will be no need to replace it. If you have an old laptop (6 years or older) it is a good idea to replace the thermal paste at least. Thermal paste can be bought online or locally at stores like Radio Shack. It is called "Arctic Silver 5 Thermal Paste" Do not buy Ceramic Thermal Paste (white-ish in color) as this is made for Desktop CPUs and not for the High Heat Laptop CPU. You must use Arctic Silver Thermal Paste or Diamond Paste if available.

Yes, I said diamond paste... They make a paste that has crushed diamond dust instead of Silver or along with the silver rather... I personally have tried this; I bought a 5g container of it. Used it on a lot of laptops and compared it to silver paste. I did not see a cooling difference in the diamond; Just a price difference. This was tested on Gaming Laptops. So, don't waste your money on diamond paste, just stick with silver paste.

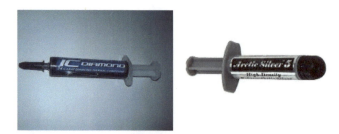

You can replace the flip chip thermal pads now too if you have a replacement pad. These can be bought online and you will need to buy the right one or it will create heating issues for your GPU (the CPU uses paste and never a pad. The GPU graphics processing unit or video chip uses a pad or paste). Most GPUs will use a pad rather than paste. The use of a pad is due to the greater amount of heat that is generated by the GPU than the CPU. The pad allows for the heat expansion and contraction and will pull heat more sufficiently than a paste will. A pad has less cooling time than a paste does. Do not use a copper shim in place of a thermal pad. I have done extensive testing on the use of shims and it will damage the upper flip chip on the GPU by applying too much pressure. It also does not allow for the natural expansion and contraction needed on the GPU like the Pad does.

This is the Laptops GPU and it will usually have a Thermal Pad.

If you must replace the pad and are not sure what thickness to get, go with a 1.5mm size.

To apply thermal paste to the CPU or the GPU, you will use the tube of thermal paste, a paper towel and a guitar pick. The most efficient way to apply the thermal paste is to press out micro dots of paste all around the silver surface of the top of the CPU chip or the GPU chipset. Start in one corner edge and work your way around making a dot about every 1mm. Then spiral the dots inward and continue placing them around until you reach the center. Do not Glob the paste on, you want a small amount on the surface.

Now you will take the guitar pick and hold it at a 20 degree angle and spread the silver paste across the top to smooth it like frosting a cake. Make sure there are no pits or uneven areas. Use the paper towel to wipe access thermal paste away. **Thats it.**

19

Notice above how there is very little paste on the flip chip pad. This is the desired results you want to see on yours as well.

You can now set aside the fan and heat

Cleaning the Motherboard

To clean the motherboard, you will need paper towel, the dry toothbrush, Q-tips or cotton swabs, Circuit board cleaner if you have it, or a cleaning solution such as Windex. If by chance you can visually see that there might be remnants of a liquid spill on the motherboard, you will be looking for any sticky substance either brown or tanish in color. You will also look for any water damage corrosion which will appear whiteish in color and possibly powdery.

If you do see evidence of this, you will want to use either Circuit Board cleaner or a can of WD-40 will work great for liquid removal. My suggestion is to go with the WD-40 as it is more readily available.

Contact & Circuit Board Cleaner

DAC-405

Electrical & Contact Cleaner

You will want to apply some of the spray onto the toothbrush, then gently dab the toothbrush on your paper towel to remove any access spray. You want the bristles just slightly damp.

Now you can brush the motherboard.

The components won't fall off by brushing over them, so don't worry.

You will use a gentle brush stroke with the toothbrush going in and out of all crevices.

Brush off the ports along the edge of the motherboard like the Ethernet input, the HDMI slot, the USB ports etc…

Yes, you will brush over these square IC chips as well; it will pull the dust from the contact feet. Clean around any capacitors (the ones shown are electrolytic capacitors.

Do not worry about being shocked (electrical) when cleaning the laptop motherboard, this is not possible as laptop motherboards are self grounded.

Cleaning the Motherboard   continued...

Please note here that you are to Never use compressed air on the laptop.

The spray will damage the motherboard. It uses a chemical solution that is not meant for circuit boards and it will create moisture under the components of the motherboard.

If you happen to come across liquid damage on the motherboard, you will want to clean that specific area with the cleaning solution (wd-40) on the toothbrush, make the toothbrush damp enough to saturate the spill area, brush vigorously to remove all traces of liquid residue.

Now use either a cotton swab (Q-tip) or a piece of folded up paper towel and dry the area of the spill by dabbing the swab or towel on the area. Also you will want to dry off the toothbrush by rubbing it on a paper towel to remove as much remaining solution on the bristles and to help dry it.

You will go over the area with the dry toothbrush now to ensure that all residue is removed and repeat the drying with a cotton swab or paper towel.

Continue cleaning the motherboard using the toothbrush, flip the board over and clean the other side the same way. You can remove the memory chips (RAM) from their slots and brush that area as well. The RAM will be locked in place with metal prongs on both sides of the RAM stick. You will pry each prong outward at the same time to release the RAM stick from the slot, it will pop up at a 45 degree angle; you just slide it outward at the same angle to remove. Reverse the process to replace the RAM, they will snap back in place.

You should now be done brushing and cleaning the motherboard, set the motherboard aside.

Cleaning the Casing Parts

You now want the bottom base casing in front of you as you will be cleaning it next.

You will need a toothbrush, cleaning solution (Windex) and paper towels.

Start with the paper towel, dampen it with some cleaning solution then wipe off the entire inside of the bottom base. Don't worry about not getting every area clean because you will then use the dry toothbrush to go over the entire area. Take the toothbrush and concentrate the cleaning in the fan exhaust ports and the perforated areas meant for heat release. Take a dampened paper towel and fold it numerous times, then you want to clean the outer edge of the bottom base where it meets the upper palm-rest. A Q-tip also works well for this. Flip the bottom base over to its bottom side, and use the toothbrush in the empty battery bay.

Now blow off any remaining dust from the bottom base.

For the upper palm-rest, you will see that the underside is generally clean. Look for the area where the fan lies and you will see a pattern of dust/debris. Clean this area with the toothbrush and a damp paper towel.

Flip the palm-rest over so the touchpad and empty keyboard bay are visible.

You will start by using your toothbrush here. Clean the inner edge of the keyboard bay, then if your palm-rest has perforated speaker holes, clean them with the toothbrush, jab the toothbrush up and down gently to poke the bristles through if needed. Now clean the touchpad outer edge. Here on some model laptops there is a minute gap between the touchpad and the rest of the palm-rest. You can use a toothpick here by running it along the touchpad's outer rim and in the gap around the touchpad. After cleaning the touchpad area, you will then continue on by cleaning the touchpad button area the same way. Move the toothbrush over the edges of the buttons being careful not to pull the button caps off. If you do happen to pull a touchpad button off while cleaning, you

24

should be able to simply press back down on the button to re-snap it back in place. Make sure the rubber contact pad is still under the button before re-snapping the button down.

You can now use a dampened paper towel to clean the rest of the palm-rest.

Removing Stickers

A good tip here for any sticker removal or sticker glue removal is to use Wd-40 on a piece of paper towel. Soak the paper towel in Wd-40 and wipe the area numerous times. If you want to remove a whole sticker – you just soak the paper of the sticker with Wd-40 and let sit for a minute, then, wipe off. You will now use dry paper towel folded a few times. Rub the area where the stickers were or are. The dry towel will pull the Wd-40 and the sticker glue away from the palm-rest. Continue by unfolding the paper towel and refolding it to expose a clean – dry spot on the paper towel, then, continue rubbing the area where the sticker is/was. You might need to repeat the process with a new damp soaked paper towel with the Wd-40. Rub it over the area; then again use a dry towel to pull all solution and residue away. You can now take a new piece of paper towel and spray it with the Windex cleaning solution. Wipe over the removed sticker area to remove any remaining Wd-40 and sticker residue.

Cleaning the Casing Parts continued…

You can now clean the media strip (the upper keyboard molding piece) if you have one.

At this point, you should now have all the lower half pieces clean. Remember to remove any SD card trays from the motherboard, clean them and put them back in their tray. Set all the lower base parts aside (motherboard, palm-rest, media strip, and bottom base) and place the keyboard in front of you.

Cleaning the Keyboard

For the keyboard cleaning, you will need the toothbrush, paper towel and the Windex or cleaning solution.

It will be important here to not get liquid under the keys.

You will start the keyboard cleaning with a dry bristled toothbrush.

Hold the toothbrush at a 45 degree angle to the keyboard, then brush along the entire row of keys. Flip the toothbrush and clean the opposite side of the key row so that the toothbrush bristles reach the top of the key and the bottom. Do the next row of keys the same way, you can go along the entire row with one swipe, or you can scrub back and forth gently all along the row. The keys are held on pretty well, so don't worry too much about popping a key off.

You want to blow on the keyboard every few swipes of the toothbrush to remove the debris. You will run the toothbrush up and down now, between the sides of the keys (all of them) then blow away the debris.

Now take a piece of paper towel and spray it with a little cleaning solution. Fold it several times and swipe very slowly across all the keys. The goal here is to just clean the tops of the keys - going slow because you don't want the paper towel to grab the edge of a key and pull it off. Once all keys have been wiped with a damp towel, use a dry towel and go over the top of the keys once more to remove any remaining liquid. You Must Make Sure Not To Dampen The Towel Too Much Or The Liquid Will Drain Off Below The Keys Onto The Keyboard Digitizer Panel and will Deteriorate the Contact Pads and Traces Causing Keyboard Failure.

There is no need to clean the underside of the keyboard, though some keyboards will have a circular dust buildup on the bottom of the keyboard that you can simply wipe away.

You can now set the keyboard aside and grab the screen for your next part to clean.

Cleaning the Screen / Disassembly of the Screen

Disassembly:

I will start here by instructing you on how to disassemble the screen. You might need to actually take it apart for a more thorough cleaning, or to fix an issue with the screen. This will show you how to replace the front frame or the rear screen cover as well.

The frame is the outer rim that surrounds the screen front panel. All laptops have one. Certain laptops (newer) will have a glass panel and or touch screen panel over the screen. If you have this type, you will not be disassembling the screen... Sorry... but these glass panels are heat-sealed to the panel and you risk the chance of cracking the touch screen or glass panel.

If you do choose to attempt a repair on these Touch Panels or outer Glass Panels, you will need to have a Heat Gun and a Suction Cup.

You can buy a simple 2 speed heat gun from your local home improvement store like Home Depot or Lowes. You will be using the Low speed/Low heat setting.

You will take your suction cup/plunger and apply it to the glass panel. Slowly heat the glass panel going around the edge of the screen panel. You will also be pulling the plunger/suction cup outward to pull the panel away. Work from a corner, and once it releases – continue around pulling the glass away. You will need to be careful when pulling the panel away as there will be a thin ribbon connection cable that is attached to the glass panel. This cable needs to be disconnected before removing the panel.

Disassembly Continued:

Now back to the screen disassembly instructions for the typical laptop screen.

Your laptop will have a front frame also called a bezel. Some are attached with both snap lock tabs and screws, and some are just snapped on with no screws (most models will typically have both screws and snap lock tabs though all will have snap lock plastic tabs). You will need your pry tool (like the guitar pick) and your mini phillips-head screwdriver to remove the front bezel. First, you will remove the screws if there are any. These screws will be covered by a plastic or rubber piece and to access the screw – you will first need to remove the screw cover. This can be tricky and you might want to use the Micro Flat head screwdriver or a razor blade for this.

I suggest using the razor blade because there is typically no room to stick the edge of a flat head screwdriver (even the micro sized ones) between the screw cover and the frame without damaging the screw cover. There will usually be 2 screws at the bottom left and right sides of the screen frame also look at the top right and left sides for 2 more screws. Some laptops will also have 2 screws in the center of the top of the frame and some will also have 2 screws at the bottom of the screen in the center of the frame. Once all screws are removed (typically all the same size), set aside and label if needed. Now you will begin to pry the plastic lock tabs to separate the front bezel from the rear screen panel.

The best place to start is the side of the frame. You will insert the pry tool between the frame piece and the rear screen cover. You can bypass the pry tool on some models and use just your fingers, I will explain… The frame snaps will pull apart if you can start from the side of the frame – grabbing the frame piece in the middle and pulling it inward towards the center of the screen and outward towards yourself at the same time – the frame will unsnap from the rear panel. This will allow you to continue pulling the frame inward and outward to unsnap the whole frame assembly.

If you use the pry tool, you will still need to pry and push slightly towards the center of the screen and outward to release the tab.

Slide the pry tool upward an inch or two and continue on popping the tabs. Once you have a good five inches of frame released, you can grab a hold of the frame and pull off the rest of the bezel away with your hands.

Set the bezel aside.

Now you will see the entire screen panel. Look at the right and left sides. There will typically be frame rails that attach to each side of the screen (some will have an upper securing bar). These frame rails will either be attached to the rear screen panel or will be just attached to the hinges at the bottom of the screen. The most common type will be just attached to the hinges. Look at the top right and left corners of the screen for any securing screws (typically there are 2 – one on each side) remove these. You will now be able to pull the top of the screen panel towards yourself an inch or two which will help you in removing the side hinge rail screws from the sides of the screen.

These screws are small so be careful not to lose them when removing them - which is why I suggest you apply an earth magnet to your screwdriver when removing screws.

You will find 2 to 4 screws on the sides of the screen that attach the screen to the side rails, the bottom screws are going to be the hardest to remove and you will need to grab a hold of the screen at the top and pull it towards yourself to allow access to the bottom screws being careful not to pull to far or you risk the chance of bending or breaking the side hinge rail(s).

Once you have removed the side rail screws, you will be able to pull the screen away. Some laptops will have a web cam cable stuck to the rear of the screen that is attached to the web cam board. You can either unplug it from the board or you can unstick it from the back of the screen to pull the screen down further. You want to just pull the screen downward from the top so you can gain access to the display cable and the display cable port on the rear side of the screen. LED screens will have the connection at the bottom of the rear of the screen and LCD (ccfl bulb) screens will have the connection at the top left side of the rear of the screen. These cables will have a piece of Sticky tape that adheres them to the input port on the rear of the screen and you will first need to unstuck this tape to allow you to pull the display cable away from its port. Make sure you pull it straight out and not at an angle.

You can now safely pull the screen away from the rear screen cover.

That is all for the screen disassembly instructions.

Cleaning the screen can be done with the screen still assembled as well. I just suggest disassembly of the screen because some people will choose to eat in front of their laptops and a lot of crumbs from food will tend to make their way into the inside of the screen frame/bezel. You will notice this if you clean off the palm rest and keyboard area, then close the lid and shake the laptop slightly, reopen the lid of the laptop and you will see that crumbs will be all over the palm rest and keyboard that have come from the inside of your screen housing. So, removing the screen and thoroughly cleaning the upper half of the laptop is recommended.

www.ingramcontent.com/pod-product-compliance
Lightning Source LLC
Chambersburg PA
CBHW041151050326
40689CB00004B/722